Marketing for Professionals.

The Handbook for Emerging Entrepreneurs in the 21ST Century

Dr. Daryl D. Green

"Dr. Green is a highly effective scholar and educator. I have known and worked with Daryl for several years and personally experienced the wonderful things an authentic, values-driven individual can achieve. This handbook will certainly be a useful resource to aspiring entrepreneurs."

Dr. Thomas Kohntopp, Program Coordinator, School of Management, Walden University

"Daryl Green has been VERY helpful to me regarding marketing for our "Kid Entrepreneurs Need Nurturing Young" book and website. He is VERY easy to understand and follow. The information he provides is a wealth of knowledge! This book will definitely be a GREAT resource for budding and current entrepreneurs."

Jacquelyn Payne
NMP Information Services (K.E.N.N.Y)
www.nmpinfo.com
www.kidentrepreneurs.biz

"Daryl Green is a clear thinking leader and strategist who studies the global markets and today's business concepts to help entrepreneurs, companies and institutions understand what it takes to survive and achieve their next level growth. 'How you finish is all that matters.'"

Terry G. Provost
Commercial and Residential Real Estate Investor

All Rights Reserved. Copyright © 2017 by Daryl D. Green

All rights reserved. Except as permitted under the Copyright Act of 1976, no part of this publication may be reproduced or distributed in any form or by any means, electronic or mechanical, including photocopying and recording, or stored on any information storage or retrieval system, without the written permission of the publisher.

Although the authors and publisher have exhaustively researched all sources to ensure the accuracy and completeness of the information contained in this book, we assume no responsibility for errors, inaccuracies, omissions, or any inconsistency herein. Anything appearing derogatory to people or organizations is unintentional. Readers should use their own judgment or an attorney or other experts for their individual concerns.

No part of this book may be reproduced or transmitted in any form or by any means, graphic, electronic, or mechanical, including photocopying, recording, taping or by any information storage or retrieval system, without the permission in writing from the publisher.

Graphic images are credited to

iStock (www.istockphoto.com) and Adobe Stock (stock.adobe.com).

Published by PMLA Press

For information on ordering in bulk, please contact:

PMLA

5322 Lance Drive

Knoxville, TN 37909

(865)602-7858

advice@darylgreen.org

TABLE OF CONTENTS

ACKNOWLEDGEMENTS	vii
PREFACE	xi
CHAPTER 1: INTRODUCTION	1
CHAPTER 2: MARKETING BASICS FOR PROFESSIONALS	5
CHAPTER 3: KNOWING YOUR COMPETITION	13
CHAPTER 4: MARKETING APPROACHES FOR ENTREPRENEURS	23
CHAPTER 5: CONCLUSION	31
ABOUT THIS EXPERT	33
REFERENCES	37
GLOSSARY	39
OTHERS MATERIALS BY DR. GREEN	41
APPENDICES	49
APPENDIX A	51
WEBSITES FOR ENTREPRENUERS	55
APPENDIX B	57
APPENDIX C	59
APPENDIX D	63
APPENDIX E	65
APPENDIX F	71
INDEXING	73

Acknowledgements

There are plenty of people to thank for the development of this project. If individuals are really successful, it is not by their own merits. I feel you need to surround yourself with a great support network. I want to thank my wife Estraletta for being patient with me on my many projects during the years of our marriage. Estraletta, you are a remarkable woman with incredible talent. In fact, I would not be successful without you. I want to also thank our immediate family—our children Mario, Sharlita, and Demetrius. You continue to supply me with plenty of love. I also want to thank my mothers'—my mother-in-law, the late Mrs. Lucy Andrews, and my dear mother, Annette Green Elias; they have continued to keep me grounded by providing sound advice.

God has blessed me with plenty of academic advisors who have guided my academic progress. Knoxville College has played a critical role in this process. I want to thank Dr. John Williams for assisting me with my first professorship. In addition, I want to thank Dr. Cannon, Dr. Grohman, and Dr. Hallman for always being supportive of my scholarly research at the college. Again, I must thank the administration at Knoxville College for allowing me the flexibility to test concepts while offering students some innovative approaches to learning. In addition, I must thank my Regent University family for giving me these vital academic tools to make a significant contribution to society. All of my doctoral professors have helped shape my worldview.

DR. DARYL D. GREEN

In particular, Dr. Bruce Winston, Dr. Bramwell Osula, and Dr. Gary Roberts have meticulously mentored me in a scholarly fashion. Special tribute goes to Lincoln Memorial University and leadership of Dean Jack McCann in assisting me in my academic development. Finally, I want to thank the Oklahoma Baptist University (OBU) for selecting me for a prestigious full-time faculty position where I can develop and grow to be all God designed me to be. My latest book represents living on this edge in a world of opportunities and uncertainties.

Clearly, an individual needs good people in order to produce that special project. I want to thank my special assistant Antoinette Kelley for her administrative support which enhanced the professionalism of this project. I must thank Bill Bailey for giving me the idea for developing this marketing book. Bill is my friend and an awesome person with great potential. Getting input from emerging professionals was invaluable. Given this fact, I want to personally thank the following graduate and undergraduates in my class at OBU: **MKTG5523-** Amina Akhabue, Gideon Asante, Nalinee Junkaew, Lakshminarayanan Kalimuthu, Robrt Marquardt, and Javier Sossa; **MKTG3303-** Caroline Abbe, Suzanne Afchain, Haley Ballard, Autumn Breckenridge, Amanda Buckwalter, Brady Clinton, Kasey Collie, Morgaan Davenport, Franklin Edwards, Grant Ericsson, Alyssa Fluke, Tyler Fuller, Tyler Harris, Allison Ingrim, Levi Jennings, Brant Kolarik, Alex Lewis, McKenzie Lumry, Gage Meisinger, Kevin Mendoza, Jade Mitchell, Kailey Moore, Alex Morales, Phillip Pelley, Josh Pettijohn, Connelly Rader, Jessica Schooler, Kadrian Shelton, Nathan Sosa, Kristijan Stunkovic, Jacob Vanderslice Erika Whited, Tucker Yarbrough, and Aaron Yount; and **MGMT3453-** Brandon Garrett, Sarah Ingle, Long

Nguyen, Ashley Olivares, Kyle Perdew, Katie Richety, Chandler Rickey, Jill Shipman, and Cheyenne Wiley. You made a difference!!!

In addition, I want to also thank the librarians, especially the Knoxville Public Library for their assistance in my research. I want also to thank everyone who read, evaluated, and commented on this book because your feedback was critical in my success. Living in the Knoxville area has afforded me great opportunities to grow as a scholar and entrepreneur. I am sure that my new home in Oklahoma will produce even greater results. I understand my accomplishments were not made alone. May God continue to bless your journey!

Preface

Marketing has so many applications to the day-to-day functions of today's Twenty-First Century citizen. This concept certainly my attention. I am always seeking ways to become a better instructor to my students. In fact, this book evolved from a course given at Knoxville College called *Introduction to Entrepreneurship*. At the time, I had students developing their own business ventures. I later followed up with a Marketing Management course the following semester. Clearly, it is easier to create a holistic approach to teaching these courses than blindly following an institution's template. How does an individual create innovation while maintaining the status quo? I am always searching for ways to improve meeting my clients' needs by providing innovation and creativity. This requires that I don't get too comfortable with the status quo. I am constantly reading, reviewing, and analyzing social and economic trends that are taking place locally as well as globally. In fact, I feel that entrepreneurs may help solve some social ills by giving individuals opportunities. Personally, I feel God has a special calling for each of us. If we fail to reach our potential in life, we are not just failing ourselves; we are failing God. Why wait on others to give you your happiness? There is no guarantee that it will happen. Therefore, I encourage people to take charge of their lives.

Marketing for Professionals provides a roadmap for steering clear of marketing landmines by focusing on market opportunities in a systematic fashion. I won't waste your time with fluffy and meaningless academic learning. What I'm sharing with you…matters! Topics include marketing strategy, competition, new product deployment, marketing mix (product, price, place, and promotion), niche markets/segmentation, and marketing analyses to name a few key topics. The purpose of this book is to provide hope in the midst of uncertainty. I hope that you can visualize your own silver lining. With a new sense of direction, I hope you will gain the financial success that you desire. Now is the perfect time to start.

CHAPTER 1

INTRODUCTION

You have a great idea. You rush to develop it and get it out to your customers. You feel it's a sure winner. Therefore, you empty out your savings account and spend it on expensive TV and magazine ads. Unfortunately, your advertising campaign gives you marginal success. Suddenly, you're broke, frustrated, and dejected. No one told you that getting people to buy was that difficult. You ponder what went wrong with your great product.

> **Successful entrepreneurs find unmet needs and capitalize on opportunities.**

With the rapid pace of technology and increasing access to information, the world is a land of opportunities for those who have the knowledge. Unfortunately, many do not know how to begin. Learning about marketing is the answer. Marketing means understanding your customer in an intimate way and satisfying their immediate needs. For example, I was riding the Metro subway in Washington, DC and got off at the end of the line. The location was in a depressed area and there was little there for the commuter. As I waited for my ride, I saw these two boys carrying a huge box of M&Ms in hopes of selling to weary commuters. I found it amusing that these young men were hustling in such a manner. Yet, this is the spirit of an entrepreneur. They had found an unmet need in the market. Yes, with no stores located in the immediate area, these young men sold a lot of M&Ms to hungry commuters. As a professor at a small college, business students often ask me how to grow a business venture. In fact, I must go beyond what the textbook states to relate to these young entrepreneurs. In this scenario, I must translate marketing theory into relevant, practical insight that can be implemented by practitioners. Clearly, marketing gives individuals the ability to understand how to locate these opportunities and what to do when you find them. Sadly, most business owners do not have the time to take a long drawn-out college course, while others want a simple process for understanding the basic concepts until they can take more formalized courses. In fact, when you don't have a lot of money to spend on advertising your product, you have to be smarter and more creative in order to stay ahead of the competition.

Marketing for Professionals provides individuals with a proven method of marketing—an easy, cost-effective way to gain influence with others. The book provides strategies, practical guidelines, resources, and a host of suggestions to help you with your business goals. This book is designed for young entrepreneurs but can help seasoned entrepreneurs, newbies, college students, managers, executives, academics, and others with a desire to grow their business dreams. For over 20 years, I have evaluated organizations so that they can be effective. At Lincoln Memorial University as an adjunct faculty, I began learning how to fully utilize management and marketing principles to assist local organizations. Since 2009, my MBA students have provided over 2500 hours of consulting time to local organizations. These major institutions include Pilot Corporation, University of Tennessee, Bechtel National, UT-Battelle, Scripps Network, Children's Hospital, Boys and Girls Club of America, Maryville College, and Shaw Environmental. I have also been involved with new startups and understand the challenges of deploying new products and services into an established market. In fact, I have seen undergraduate students in my classes develop new start-ups and become successful. Thus, you can learn how to use these marketing skills with little or no formal training in marketing concepts. You just need to have a willing spirit to learn new ideas.

DR. DARYL GREEN'S
NEW PRODUCT DEVELOPMENT MODEL FOR SAVVY ENTREPRENEURS

1. Determine your core competencies (what you do well) and flowchart how you can transform those qualities into a sellable product/service.
2. Evaluate the targeted industry/market.
3. Locate the market leaders and benchmark from them (i.e. taking the best processes from them and improving your product/service).
4. Identify primary competitors as well as some indirect competition to gauge the market.
5. Select your specific product/service.
6. Develop your value proposition/unique selling position. What value are you providing to customers? Why should they buy from you instead of your competitors?
7. Write a description of your potential buyers (i.e. demographics, social standing, etc.).
8. Create an appealing product name that tells customers what you are offering.
9. Write a product/service description.
10. In a crowded market where sellers are offering similar products, you should develop a niche strategy. In fact, developing your own new product/service category would be preferred. Example – DELL Computers with online computer ordering
11. Develop a simple marketing strategy that captures how you plan to execute your product offering in the marketplace.
12. Test your product/services with prospective buyers (i.e. focus group) and use the feedback to improve your product.
13. Build enthusiasm around your product launching with promotional activities including a media release.
14. Launch new product and monitor customers response. Track results.
15. Review results to enhance future product/service offerings.

WWW.DRDARYLGREEN.COM

CHAPTER 2

MARKETING BASICS FOR PROFESSIONALS

Working in the engineering field for over 25 years, I was always fond of solving problems for others. In fact, I have developed a passion for product development. Build a great product and people will come knocking at your door. This was the mentality of the business world for several decades. In fact, companies were product-focused. They made the product, in many cases without customer input, and then tried to find buyers for these products. Of course, hindsight is 20/20. Today it is clear that this is not the best strategy for an organization attempting to make a profit. Therefore, effective marketing requires a new mechanism for entrepreneurs to become more successful. According to the American Marketing Association, marketing can be defined as an organizational function and a set of processes for creating, capturing, communicating, and delivering value to customers.[1] However, the simplest definition is that marketing is about understanding and satisfying customer wants or needs. In fact, there are times when customers do not know what they want or desire.

> **Sadly, many people underestimate the difficulty of understanding customers.**

Loaded with plenty of energy and enthusiasm, some entrepreneurs launch out to start a business with little knowledge about their market. Passion is great! Yet, a passionate person with little experience about the marketing process can be a fatal mistake. For example, Will Carter is a senior manager at the top of his career in the oil industry. There's economic downturn in the oil industry. Companies started downsizing workers. Will is no exception. Will takes his severance and invests in a life-long dream being a of restaurant owner. Initially, the restaurant is a success with the assistance of Will's family, friends, and his former co-workers. As the financial downturn continues, individuals start eating at home. Will's restaurant closed within

---

1 *Marketing* by Dhruv Grewal and Michael Levy

five years. Dealing with a bad boss and a hostile work environment, Betty Smith longed to start her own business. Eventually, Betty found the nerve to resign from her consulting business and open her firm. Betty had lots of confidence and passion. She was the most sought after consultant at her firm because of her problem solving ability. As Betty started her life as business owner, she found that running a business was not easy. She did not know how to sell or network to gain contracts. Thus, Betty spent lots of her time pursuing unprofitable leads. Within five years, Betty accepted a senior consultant position with a small firm while closing her own business. Sadly, the landscape of new businesses is riddled with passionate individuals who know nothing about marketing concepts.

Consequently, marketing becomes that linchpin in the process of finding a solution for consumers. Traditionally, marketing has been defined in terms of four variables described as the marketing mix, or the 4Ps: product/service, price, placement, and promotion. In fact, the marketing mix is the controllable set of activities that entrepreneurs use to attract or respond to the needs of their target market. In essence, entrepreneurs attempt to create value for their customers. Value relates to the customer viewpoint, not that of the business. Value relates to the benefit the customer perceives they are getting in exchange for their purchase of the product or service. Given this reality, selling must develop a unique selling proposition for buyers.

Business experts Donald Lehmann and Russell Winer point out that inaccurate information or incorrect analysis often leads to poor decisions about marketing a business product.[2] This flaw can hurt a

---

2 *Analysis for Marketing Planning* by Donald Lehman and Russell Winer

business attempting to make a profit. In fact, understanding competition is a point most executives miss. Some of the marketing questions to ponder include:

- What is your marketing strategy?
- What is the value of your product/service to customers?
- What is your positioning strategy?
- What markets do you currently own and what is the future outlook?
- How do you distinguish your products from those of your competition?

Savvy entrepreneurs understand the importance of marketing to a target market instead of random selling. Gordon Burgett, niche-marketing guru, uses a method called Targeting, Customizing, and Expanding (TCE). His approach requires novel methods of bringing a product to the market. It is not an internally-focused approach where an individual builds his products and hopes to locate an appropriate market. Rather, the TCE process first clearly defines the market, then distributes directly to customers, and finally seeks to build effective relationships so that a further expansion of products and services is possible. Targeting means to find a group of potential buyers with a need; an entrepreneur seeks to help them solve their needs. In following this scenario, an entrepreneur must determine if there are enough qualified buyers. This is what marketing to a niche market means.

Global Market

Entrepreneurs search for opportunities. In fact, the biggest opportunities are abroad. Therefore, entrepreneurs should understand the dynamics of dealing with a global market. The international market continues to grow. Communication technology and the Internet bring international communities together. Where there are opportunities, there is profit to be made. Ask the major companies. Using the PEST Analysis is a logical method for entering a global market; it focuses on political, economic, socio-cultural, and technological factors of a targeted country.

Robert Taft, author of *Growing Your Business Globally*, explains that large corporations have traditionally dominated international business, with over 70 percent of the total value of America's exports in 2000.[3] However, small and medium-size companies accounted for an increase of over 300 percent in the total number of American exporters in the 1990s. During this time frame, five key industries (consumer goods, automotive manufacturing, aircraft manufacturing, electronics components, and steels) controlled 50 percent of the world markets. Let's analyze this international market. The global economy is made up of 232 countries that are culturally diverse in many different ways.

Starting in the early 1990s, more countries started to open up to free trade. Obviously, a business needs to do its homework to determine if a product or service will do well internationally as well as domestically. A product that does well in America may fail in Canada even

---

3 *Growing Your Business Globally* by Robert Taft

though the cultures are similar. Taft advocates that a potential small business should (a) evaluate its ability to export, (b) plan adequately so that execution is feasible, and (c) prepare a strategy to understand the target market and expand overseas, if needed. However, there are many perils in dealing with markets internationally, such as international trade laws, government restrictions, shipping issues, currency challenges, and a host of communication problems. From our evaluation, using an established partner is the preferred method of operations to promote success in international markets.

Entrepreneurial Spirit

Entrepreneurs are individuals who are willing to take risk for financial gain by starting something new. In fact, they are more than just business owners or managers. Being normal is not a word that can be commonly used for an entrepreneur. Clearly, they walk to a different beat, and this is what makes them so interesting in America. If you are only interested in "me," then this is not the approach for you. Entrepreneurs focus on solving market problems; good results produce wealth, influence, and power. Entrepreneurs are typically described as innovators, inventors, mavericks, or just counterculture individuals. In fact, studies have shown that entrepreneurs have a different set of values than other people when it comes to starting a business. Clearly, entrepreneurs must track markets so that they can take advantage of any window of opportunity. Therefore, entrepreneurs must understand marketing, what it is and what it is not. Limited by financial capital, many entrepreneurs are forced to be resourceful. When individuals have limited capital for marketing, out-the-box thinking must exist. Guerrilla marketing provides innovative thinking to marketing by focusing on low-cost unconventional marketing tactics that attracts buyers while catching traditional marketers off guard. In his 1984 book, *Guerrilla Advertising*, Jay Conrad Levinson coined guerilla marketing as a way for small businesses and entrepreneurs to compete against the establishment.[4] Individuals needed to possess the primary competitive advantages in guerilla marketing which are their passion, high energy, and internal drive to success in the market. Levinson noted about guerrilla marketing: "Every component that helps you sell what you are selling is part of the marketing process. No detail is too insignificant to be included.

The more you realize that, the better your marketing will be. Robert Hisrich, Michael Peters, and Dean Shepherd, authors of *Entrepreneurship*, further argued that entrepreneurs conduct the following steps (whether formally or informally) in starting a new business venture: (a) identify and evaluate the opportunity, (b) develop a business strategy, (c) determine the required resources, and (d) manage the resulting enterprise. Therefore, effective entrepreneurs pay close attention to their potential customers, their competitors, and relevant trends in order to launch a successful venture.[5] In spite of any good planning approach, a business will not be successful without an effective marketing strategy. Thus, a business owner or entrepreneur's understanding of marketing is a critical component for successful operations.

---

4 What is Guerrilla Marketing? By Creativityguerillamarketing.com
5 *Entrepreneurship* by Robert Hsirick, Michael Peters, and Dean Shepherd

Positioning Strategy Facts

Positioning Strategy Secrets:

- ❖ General Market - a generic set of potential buyers who may or may not be interested in your product or service.
- ❖ Target Market - specific set of qualified customers who are interested in your product or service.

CHAPTER 3

KNOWING YOUR COMPETITION

As many Millennials start flooding the employment landscape, young adults are considering starting their own businesses. Corporate downsizing and layoffs have thrust many individuals into a tough employment market while other employed workers who are dissatisfied with their jobs plot to implement a plausible exit strategy which will land them in their ideal job. Sadly, many people run with these well intended ideas about starting a business but with little insight into how to implement their plan so that the idea can be successful. Most folks don't realize that there is nothing new under the sun and that they would find someone else who is doing what they set out to do. In fact, some people find themselves in a highly competitive environment with little or no plan for navigating this climate. In this chapter, we will examine the concepts of competition for small businesses. Individuals will learn more about starting a business in a competitive environment.

The small business sector is quickly dominating the landscape in most local communities. Individuals who start their own businesses take control of their financial future. With technology and the Internet, today's business owners enjoy more access to information and experts to assist in their endeavors. According to the U.S. Small Business Association, U.S. small businesses make-up about 54% (28 million) of all U.S. sales. Since 1970s, small businesses provide 55% of all jobs and 66% of all net new jobs.[6] While the corporate landscape has been contracting, small business "start-ups" have grown. Since the 90s, the small businesses sector has added 8 million new jobs.[7] Realistically speaking, some individuals are not good candidates for new start-ups because their personality is built on someone telling them what to do. We call this an external locus of control where the individual does not

---

6   " Small business trends" by U.S. SBA
7   " Small business trends" by U.S. SBA

have control of their lives; things happen to them as a matter of luck or chance.[8]

Today's generation of business owners have this strong internal locus to drive their business ideas. Tech savvy Millennials are set to cause many to rethink what it means to start a new business from scratch. According to the 2016 BNP Paribas Global Entrepreneur Report, Millennials are embracing entrepreneurship as a way of life faster than their Baby Boomer parents.[9] A study was conducted with 2,600 entrepreneurs in 18 countries, in Asia, Europe, and the United States. The researchers of this study, Scorpio Partnership, discussed the emergence of new entrepreneurs less than 35 years old called "The Millenniprenuers" born between 1980 and 1995. Comparing Millennials to Baby Boomers, the study showed an increased number of companies, both in the new economy and traditional sectors for Millennials. They launched about eight companies on the average compared with 3.5 by Baby Boomers. In fact, Millennials have a turnover of 43% more than their Baby Boomer counterparts.[10]

> **Entrepreneurs are cut from a different cloth with a high internal locus of control; they feel that their actions play a strong part in their destiny.**

Small businesses must understand the tenets of competition. According to Businessdictionary.com, competition can be defined as "rivalry in which every seller tries to get what other sellers are seeking at the same time: sales, profit, and market share by offering

---

8 *Leadership* by Richard Daft
9 "2016 BNP Paribas Global Entrepreneur Report" by Scorpio Partnership
10 "2016 BNP Paribas Global Entrepreneur Report" by Scorpio Partnership

the best practical combination of price, quality, and service." The competitive environment should be considered when planning a business venture. In general, there are four basic climates for business environments which include monopoly, oligopoly, pure competition, and monopolistic competition.[11] In a monopoly, the company is the sole provider where competitors are non-existent. This situation is highly favorable to start-ups and very rare. One example of a monopoly would be utility companies in small, local areas. Most businesses operate in a pure competition or oligopoly where businesses with similar products and services compete for the same customers who have an array of options before them.

Given this scenario, businesses must work harder to attract customers by attempting to differentiate their offerings from their competitors. Lastly, in a monopolistic environment, different companies offer products and services that make customers see the differences. In fact, businesses seek to build a niche (monopoly) where they can control a specific target market.[12] One good example would be Dell Companies entry into the computer industry. Instead of entering the computer business and facing IBM, the market leader head on, Dell Company utilized niche strategy by having customers place their company orders online, phone, or fax. This concept caught IBM off guard and revolutionized how computers were sold in the industry.[13]

---

11   *Essentials of Marketing* by William Perreault, Joseph Cannon, and Jerome McCarthy
12   *Essentials of Marketing* by William Perreault, Joseph Cannon, and Jerome McCarthy
13   "Market entry strategies: pioneers versus late arrivals" by Gurumurthy Kalyanaram and Ragu Gurumurthy

Unfortunately, some new business start-ups do not spend enough time thinking about their market and the level of competition they will face. That reality is a tragic mistake for many businesses. According to a 2015 Forbes column, nine out of ten new start-up businesses fail.[14] Most new companies would do well to avoid stiff competition at the onset or at least spend the necessary time in evaluating the competitive environment before entering the market. Management guru Dr. Michael E. Porter notes the importance of planning out a business strategy for success: "If all you're trying to do is essentially the same thing as your rivals, then it's unlikely that you'll be very successful." Thus, the initial step of a competitor analysis is to identify potential competitors and then compare your current marketing strategy (i.e. marketing mix) with what other competitors are doing or likely to do in response to your actions in this particular market.

Dr. William Perreault, Dr. Joseph Cannon, and Dr. Jerome McCarthy, authors of *Essential of Marketing* argue for strong strategies to combat market competition: "So marketing managers should actively seek sustainable competitive advantage, a marketing mix that customers see as better than a competitor's mix and cannot be quickly or easily copied."[15] Additionally, Dr. Porter has spent his whole career analyzing strategy and competition in various industries. Competitive environments should not be taken lightly. In 1979, Harvard Business School professor Michael Porter developed a model to help explain

---

14 "90% of startups fail: Here's what you need to know about the 10% by Neil Patel

15 *Essentials of Marketing* by William Perreault, Joseph Cannon, and Jerome McCarthy

how businesses could be more profitable faced with competition.[16] Porter's Five Forces provides a method for analyzing competition for the entrepreneur or business owner; Porter's approach reviews the following five driving forces related to competitive power: (a) Threat of intense competitive rivalry, (b) Threat of new entrants, (c) Threat of buyer's growing bargaining power, (d) Threat of substitution, and (e) Threat of suppliers' growing power.[17] (See Figure 1.)

This competitive model can be a strategic tool for organizations to evaluate the attractiveness and profitability of marketing strategies in varying industry sectors.[18] *Threat of competitive rivalry* involves the climate of competition. A market is unattractive if it already contains numerous, strong, or aggressive competitors.[19] In a purely competitive environment, profitability approaches zero. Businesses in high rivalry provide a cutthroat environment where competitors go head to head for customers at any cost. Thus, businesses seek to go where there are few competitors and where they have a decisive advantage. *Threat of new entrants* is high when both entry and exit barriers are low, businesses easily enter and exit the market. When both entry and exit barriers are high, established businesses often get the most profitability.[20] Yet, when entry barriers are low and exit barriers are high, businesses are allowed to enter but exiting is extremely costly.

---

16 "Porter's Five Forces: Analyzing the Competition" by Katherine Arline
17 "Porter's Five Forces: Assessing the Balance of Power in a Business Situation" by Mindtools.com
18 "How to use Porter's Five Forces" by Annmarie Hanlon
19 *Essentials of Marketing* by William Perreault, Joseph Cannon, and Jerome McCarthy
20 *Marketing Management* by Phillip Kotler and Kevin Keller

PORTER'S FIVE FORCES MODEL

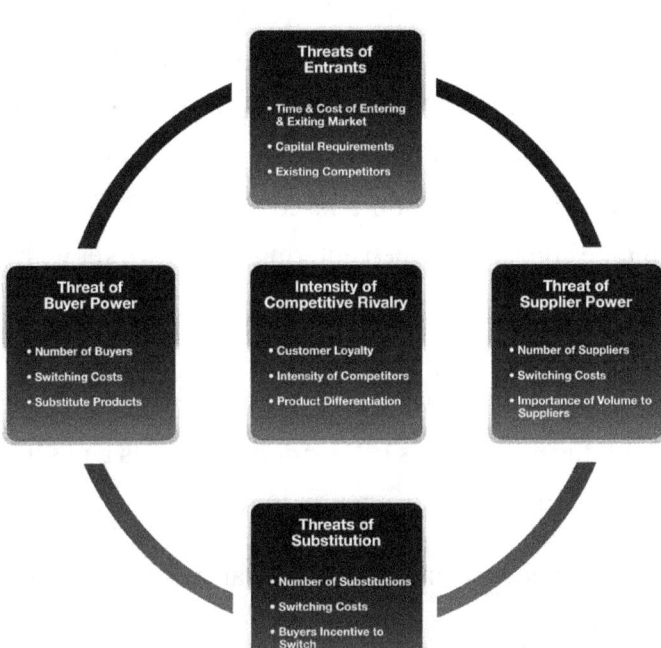

This figure is based on Dr. Michael Porter's Five Forces of Competitive Position Model

Figure 1

Threat of buyers' bargaining power notes that a market is unattractive if buyers possess strong or growing bargaining power. Buyer power is strongest when customers are organized, concentrated, or well informed and the products and services are undifferentiated. [21] *Threat of substitution* become problematic to sellers when there are actual or potential substitutes for the sellers' products which cut into prof-

---
21   *Marketing Management* by Phillip Kotler and Kevin Keller

its. *Threat of suppliers' bargaining power* happens when a market becomes unattractive and when a business' suppliers are able to raise prices or reduce quantities supplied. When suppliers are concentrated or organized, they are most powerful because the seller has limited or no other suppliers for fulfillment. [22] Given these competitive environments, small businesses and start-ups must evaluate their competitors as well as the attractiveness of proposed markets. The following questions should be considered when entering a new market with potential competition:

- What is the level of competition in the potential market?

- Do all the competitors offer similar products and services where there is little differentiation?

- Can other new businesses easily start-up with little cost or experience?

- Are there rules, regulations, or certifications that make it difficult for new businesses to easily enter?

- Are there barriers for entry that give you a distinct advantage over new competitors?

- Is it a market where there are few buyers so that they have more influence to dictate terms and conditions to sellers?

- Do buyers have other alternatives to your product or services? Are those substitutes cheaper or more convenient than your product or services?

---

22 *Marketing Management* by Phillip Kotler and Kevin Keller

- Is it a market where there are limited suppliers for your products so that suppliers have more influence in impacting your bottom line?

In a world described by hypercompetitiveness, small business and new start-ups need to understand how to build strategies that provide market advantages. Understanding how competitors act and react goes to this market advantage. In this chapter, we demonstrated how small businesses that understand the nature of competition will have a better chance of being successful in a crowded marketplace. By doing the detailed competitive analysis, new businesses can be more successful in the long run.

CHAPTER 4

MARKETING APPROACHES FOR ENTREPRENEURS

An entrepreneur can't afford simply to maintain the status quo. However, moving forward in new ventures with an unfocused marketing plan is simply foolish. Stanley Gryskiewicz, author of *Positive Turbulence*, argues that these uncertain times can generate creativity and innovation from businesses that are prepared. He explains, "What is needed to turn the turbulence into a positive force is knowledge management. This means putting structures in place for bringing in new information, making sense of it, and turning it into novel ideas that are useful and eventually can be implemented.[23]" Guerrilla Marketing provides the best approach for entrepreneurs to break into new markets, establishing themselves, or sustaining market success in an unstable environment. Jay Conrad Levinson is the Godfather of non-traditional approaches. His concept of Guerrilla Marketing levels the playing field for inspired entrepreneurs who lack the capital of large corporations. The critical component of this approach is breaking down your customers into a manageable group; focus on a target market. By using this approach, an individual is not wasting his or her time launching a marketing campaign that is unfocused and untargeted.

Jennifer and Peter Sander, niche market experts, maintain, "Find a niche in which you can build your own unique stronghold, attracting, and maintaining customers who will pay top dollar for your goods or services." Clearly, I am talking about an innovative and creative process but also a systematic and logical process. Many traditional organizations would argue that many entrepreneurs do not have the discipline to be logical and innovative. They are wrong!

From my experience, research, and review of renowned experts, the following represents a systematic approach to marketing for professionals (See Figure 2).

---

23   *Positive Turbulence* by Stanley Gryskiewicz

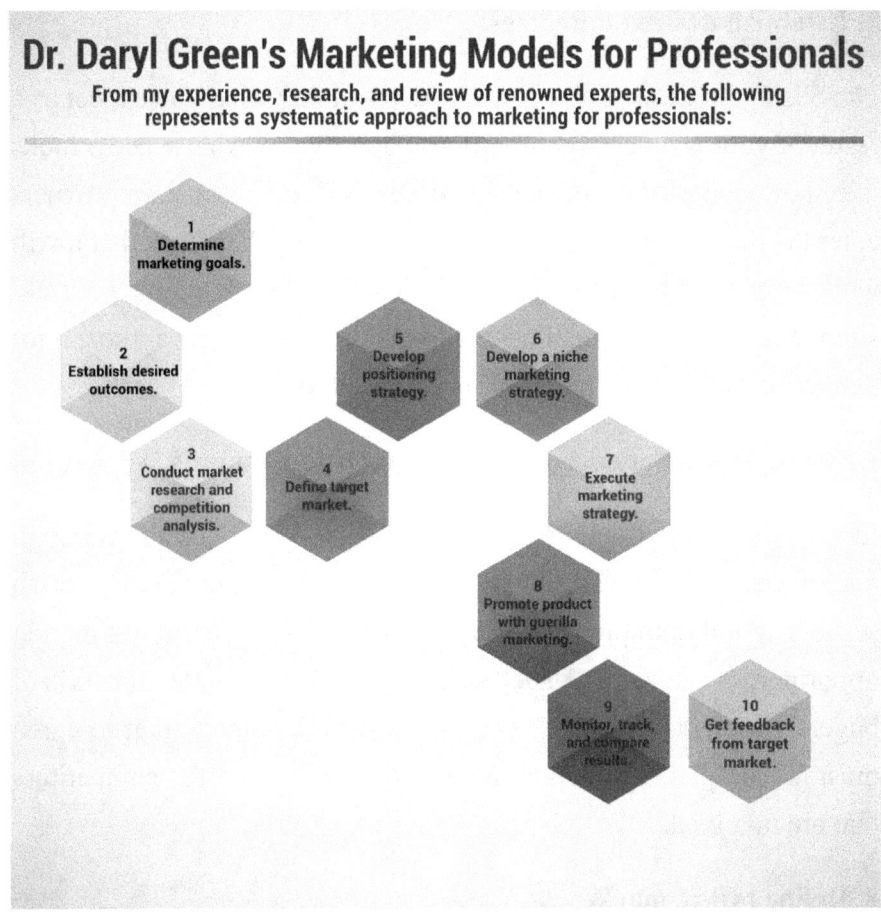

Figure 2

1. Determine marketing goals.

Effective entrepreneurs identify their business objectives up front. What do you hope to accomplish in your venture? Wealth? Market dominance? Renowned expertise? It's important to answer this question up front and build it into your strategy.

2. Establish desired outcomes.

Establish your desired outcomes by determining what you expect as a result of your business venture. If you don't know what success looks like, how can you expect to be successful? Many business owners enter the financial world with zero expectations. They hope that it will work out. However, niche marketing requires that you give your desired outcome more thought. It will help determine your approach for marketing and what level of effort you need to apply.

3. Conduct market research and competition analysis.

Identifying market opportunities can be achieved with thorough market research. In fact, identifying market opportunities is a sixth sense of good entrepreneurs. Several methods of identifying market opportunities can be used, such as trend monitoring or identification of buyers' problems. Once this step is completed, more market research must be completed to define the general market and the competitors that are involved.

4. Define target market.

With the market research completed, narrow your market by focusing on buyers who can best benefit from your products or services. Good entrepreneurs do not waste their time on suspect markets. In fact, Burget argues that a lucrative market will produce the following characteristics: (a) continual growth of the market, (b) a quick turnover of its members, or (c) a steady development of new needs. Matching an appropriate product or service to a market need is the foundation of niche marketing for entrepreneurs.

5. Develop positioning strategy.

Entrepreneurs understand that there is always competition for customers. However, most forget the fight is not a physical fight to obtain customers, but a mental process. Al Ries and Jack Trout, positioning gurus, explain, "Positioning is not what you do to a product. Positioning is what you do to the mind of the prospect." Therefore, young entrepreneurs must win the minds of their customers.[24] In fact, they must decide how they want to be perceived by their market. This self-evaluation is not done in a vacuum. Several questions must be answered. Who are the leaders in the market? How are they perceived in the minds of customers? How do customers view your organization? Can you change the mindset of this market? Therefore, entrepreneurs need to seriously develop a good positioning strategy.

6. Develop a niche marketing strategy.

Entrepreneurs can't waste time on unproductive markets. Therefore, the key to your niche marketing strategy is to take a systematic approach to introducing and positioning a new product or service. Individuals should carefully conduct relevant analysis, such as SWOT or PEST. Many business owners fail without a good plan. However, effective business people use a plan for implementing their business.

7. Execute marketing strategy.

All the good plans in the world cannot make up for faulty execution. In fact, the purpose of a marketing strategy should be to radically influence the minds and behavior of your target market.

---

[24] *Positioning* by Al Ries and Jack Trout

8. Promote product with guerilla marketing.

Guerilla Marketing is all about innovation, creativity, and energy. If you don't have a huge marketing budget, these traits provide a market advantage. Publicity is the principal tool with targeted advertising. In fact, your promotion campaign takes advantage of over a hundred guerrilla weapons available for use in forming client relationships. Young entrepreneurs should seek to speak and talk about their products or services in any venues where they find their target markets. By submitting articles to website content providers, you will be able to increase your presence on the NET with these links. You can build a presence in a newsgroup or discussion board to build long-term relationships with the target market. Referrals are three times more likely to buy from you than from direct selling. Your friendly network is transformed into online advocates in your interest. Viral marketing encourages other people to spread your marketing message and increase your exposure exponentially. Entrepreneurs should continuously network with individuals to showcase their business. By combining techniques such as article writing and viral emails, "word-of-mouth" promotions will be strategically increased.

9. Monitor, track, and compare results.

Entrepreneurs stay connected with their market. They understand that the market can quickly evaporate. By monitoring their customers, successful entrepreneurs stay ahead of their competition. These effective individuals understand that you must go back to your strategy to determine if you are being successful. Do you understand when you have reached your desired outcome for your business? Effective young entrepreneurs understand that strategies are dynamic and must be monitored and changed.

10. Get feedback from target market.

Feedback is everything in a world of uncertainty. Again, entrepreneurs don't take this for granted. They don't mind negative feedback from customers or good things said about their competition. It provides an avenue whereby they can continue to get better. Taking polls, surveys, and asking questions of customers are good ways to stay connected and improve for young entrepreneurs.

CHAPTER 5

CONCLUSION

Operating in a time of rapid change and global competition, young entrepreneurs cannot afford to lose their innovative and creative advantage in the market. Some individuals take a chance without any marketing know-how and launch a new business venture. They fail. Others recognize the importance of marketing but have little time to take a formal course geared for entrepreneurs. In doing nothing, entrepreneurs take the chance of not being profitable in a hypercompetitive environment.

> *Marketing for Professionals* can be used as a virtual guide for steering clear of the numerous mistakes made by large corporations and unprepared entrepreneurs.

However, there is no need to despair. Many marketing books deal with the market as a static and predictable environment. In fact, few books narrow in on the needs of today's young entrepreneurs. Yet, everyone knows that today's markets cannot be characterized in this manner. Our marketing environment is filled with many unknowns and uncertainty. This book provides young entrepreneurs a systematic approach to dealing with this uncertainty. As an educated entrepreneur, you can look forward to making your dreams come alive. Character does count. Use the famous motto: 'Work smarter not harder' to strategically plan out your business success. It takes persistence, commitment, passion, and vision to become successful. In addition, this book provides a process for starting, growing, and sustaining a successful business in a changing environment. Start today and achieve your desired outcome!

About this Expert

Dr. Daryl D. Green, DSL, is a management strategist who deals with a variety of complex projects. He is the Dickinson Chair of Business professor at Oklahoma Baptist University in the Paul Dickinson College of Business.

In 2016, Dr. Green retired from the Department of Energy where he worked in the Environmental Management Program for over 27 years. Before his 30th birthday, he had already managed over 400 projects, estimated at $100 million dollars. His technical experience includes program management, engineering, project management, waste management, environmental restoration, research and development, marketing, and technology transfer. He has over 25 years of assisting organizations and individuals with making good decisions.

Dr. Green is a man of Faith and believes anything is possible with God on your side. He is been an active member of Payne Avenue Missionary Baptist Church in Knoxville, Tennessee. He is an ordained deacon, bible lecturer, and youth advisor. He's been featured presenter for several organizations including Cedine Bible Camp and Knoxville Baptist District. He has over 20 years of leadership experience in religious environments and over 20 years of assisting organizations in decision-making.

His primary research is in leadership, management, culture, and decision-making. Dr. Green has contributed to the scholarly research in his discipline with more than 15 articles published in noted academic journals. Additionally, Dr. Green is a member of editorial boards in several academic journals including Strategic Leadership Review and Management and Economics Research Journal.

For his literary contribution to society, Dr. Green was recognized as one of the first recipients of the Amber Communications Group, Inc. / Blacks in Government – Greater Orange County Chapter's Annual Literary Awards. He is the author of several books and writes a syndicated online column on contemporary issues. Over 3,000 online publishers/content providers have used his articles around the globe. His *FamilyVision* column is syndicated through the National Newspaper Publishers Association and has reached over 200 newspapers and more than 15 million readers across the country. Additionally, Dr. Green has been noted and quoted by *USA Today, Ebony Magazine,* and the *Associated Press*. He has also been a freelance writer and guest columnist for various publications, including *Knoxville News Sentinel, Knoxville Enlightener, Discovery Magazine,* and the *IEEE Technology and Society Magazine*. He has also been a special assignment reporter for the *BIG Bulletin/Reporter*.

His professional experience includes management, engineering, research and development, marketing, and personal coaching. He received a B.S. in mechanical engineering from Southern University and a MA in organizational management from Tusculum College. Dr. Green received a doctoral degree in strategic leadership from Regent University. He is a past talk show host, a nationally recognized lecturer, nationally syndicated columnist, and personal advisor. These experiences place him in a unique position for understanding emerging trends.

If you would like to meet with him personally or would like more information about his services, please contact:

Dr. Daryl Green
5322 Lance Drive
Knoxville, TN 37909
Phone: (865) 602-7858
Email: advice@darylgreen.org
Home page: www.drdarylgreen.com

REFERENCES

101 Ways to Promote Yourself by Raleigh Pinksey

Analysis for Marketing Planning by Donald Lehman and Russell Winer

Consumer Behavior and the Practice of Marketing by Kenneth Runyon

Entrepreneurship by Robert Hisrich, Michael Peters, and Dean Shepherd

Everything You Need to Know to Write, Publish, & Market Your Book by Patrika Vaughn

Guerrilla Marketing by Jay Conrad Levinson

Marketing by Dhruv Grewal and Michael Levy

Marketing Management by Phil Kotler and Kevin Keller

Niche and Grow Rich by Jennifer and Peter Sander

Niche Marketing by Gordon Burgett

Positive Turbulence by Stanley Gryskiewicz

Publishing to Niche Markets by Gordon Burgett

Relationship Marketing by Regis McKenna

What is Guerrilla Marketing? By Creativityguerillamarketing.com

GLOSSARY

Brand – This term involves a name, term, sign, symbol, design, or combination of elements intended to identify the product/service with seller(s) from their competition.

Competition - The rivalry that exists between companies selling similar products and services with the goal of achieving revenue, profit, and market-share growth.

Competitive Advantage – A company's ability to perform in one or more ways that a competitor cannot or will not match.

Direct Marketing – The use of consumer-direct channels to reach and deliver products and services to customers without using middlemen.

Forecasting – The art of anticipating what buyers are likely to do under a given set of conditions.

Guerrilla Marketing is a marketing strategy that focuses on low-cost unconventional tactics that is fueled by high energy and imagination. Jay Conrad Levinson coined this term in his 1984 book *'Guerrilla Advertising.'*

Life-Cycle Cost – The product's purchase cost plus the discounted cost of maintenance and repair less the discounted salvage value.

Market – This element is a medium that allows buyers and sellers of a specific good or service to interact in order to facilitate an exchange.

Marketing – The activity, set of institutions, and processes for creating, communicating, delivering, and exchanging offerings that have value of customers, clients, partners, and society at large.

Marketing Mix – This element involves a combination of factors that can be controlled by a company to influence consumers to purchase its products.

Market Share – The concept is a higher level of selective demand of a product.

Niche Market - A niche market is the subset of the market on which a specific product/service is focused.

Target Market – This element involves a particular group of consumers at which a product or service is aimed.

Unique Selling Position (USP) - The seller's compelling reason that customers should purchase this product/service over the competition.

Value – The worth of the product/service that buyers are willing to purchase the item. Value is the difference between a prospective customer's evaluation of the benefits and costs of one product when compared with others.

OTHERS MATERIALS BY DR. GREEN

Dr. Green continues to research and produce information that aims to improve society. Below is a synopsis of some of his other products:

A Call to Destiny: How to Create Effective Ways to Assist Black Boys in America provides a practical assessment of what happens to young black boys in America. It seeks to provide ways for parents, educators, and supporters to assist these boys in their positive development. Without any intervention, young black boys, regardless of their social class, will not survive in the 21st century. In this book, A Call to Destiny, you will (a) examine the severity of the problems facing young black boys, (b) learn new strategies to bring solutions to your child and the community at large, and (c) provide inspiration to continue the fight to save this generation of boys. (Paperback: 50 pages, ISBN-13: 978-1442181021)

Awakening the Talents Within is a powerful, step-by-step approach that individuals can use to solve problems and contribute to their overall success. This book is a wake-up call for the next generation of leaders.

Green uses his charismatic style for today's hip hop culture, dealing with a wide range of issues, from stopping procrastination to creating business ownership. The solutions contained in the book reflect more than ten years of managing, consulting, and teaching in government, nonprofit, business, and private and academic institutions. (Paperback: 136 pages, ISBN: 978-0595146130, Hardcover: 140 pages, ISBN: 978-0595745722)

Book Publishing for Professionals provides the secrets of gaining this useful power. Packed with proven insights and advice, this book provides a simple, logical step-by-step process for professionals. It includes effective writing tools, best publishing options, and marketing strategies to make your book successful in the marketplace. It is geared toward the writer who wants to write a non-fiction book (biography, cookbook, self-help, Christian book, textbook, etc.).

(Paperback: 68 pages, ISBN: 978-1449985561, Kindle: 68 pages ASIN: B0047T7DPA, Workbook Hardcover: 108pages, ISBN: 978-0557983469, Workbook Paperback: 100 pages, ISBN: 978-1453898819, DVD: 26 minutes, ASIN: B001FB4Z3G, CD: 26 minutes, ASIN: B004CYFBBS)

MARKETING FOR PROFESSIONALS

Great Customer Service: The Definitive Handbook for Today's Successful Business, co-authored with Jalene Nemec, provides a framework for businesses that want sustainable success during an unstable economy. The book appeals to salespeople and anyone who wants to maintain good relationships with their customers. Readers can ensure success by following the practical application of concepts outlined in the book in order to satisfy customers' needs or wants. The book addresses the topics of building a more profitable business, increasing good sustainable customer service, inspiring workers toward great organizational performance, and learning how to inspire demanding customers. (Paperback: 148 pages, ISBN: 978-1480054707)

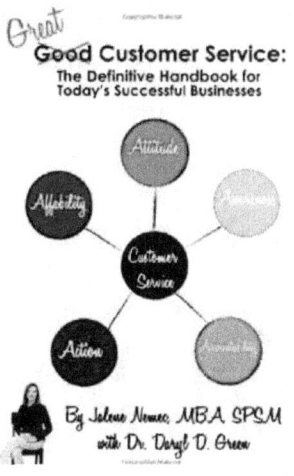

Breaking Organizational Ties provides practical strategies for employees attempting to cope in jobs or environments which they hate. While most managers are only concerned with the bottom line, they leave their employees vulnerable to the casualties of competitive markets. This book will enable readers to (a) learn how to survive and even enjoy your time at work even in a hostile environment, (b) gain greater confidence in your ability to grow while in a downsizing

organization, and (c) discover the insight to go beyond your limitations by breaking the barriers of your self-doubt. (Paperback: 124 pages, ISBN: 978-1450511315, eBook: 124 pages, Format: PDF, Hardcover: 124 pages, ISBN: 978-0557388714)

Don't be an Old Fool: Common Sense & Gratitude is a collection of Dr. Green's syndicated columns throughout the years. The book offers practical strategies for individuals who desire to make better decisions in their lives by using sound common sense approaches. With a new sense of direction, individuals will be able to re-energize themselves for the future. (Hardcover: 134 pages, ISBN: 978-0971400894, Paperback: 186 pages, ISBN: 978-1475259117)

Second Chance presents nonprofit organizations with a way to use operations management tools to make them more efficient and better equipped to assist their clients and constituents in meeting their needs. Dr. Green co-authored with one of his students. Through the eyes of student Noriko Chapman, readers will be taken on a magical journey of overcoming a difficult situation in operations management and life. (Paperback: 130 pages, ISBN: 978-1461146070)

MARKETING FOR PROFESSIONALS

Impending Danger: The Federal Handbook for Rethinking Leadership in the 21st Century provides critical answers regarding how government leaders can reduce partisan bickering by changing the current leadership paradigm. With forty years' worth of experience in the public sector, Dr. Green and his co-author Dr. Gary Roberts know what they're talking about. They made sure that the book provides revelations and insights regarding political strife and the answers that can solve them. (Hardcover: 146 pages, ISBN: 978-1607971382)

Job Strategies for the 21st Century: How to Assist Today's College Students during Economic Turbulence provides practical solutions to the challenges that today's college students face when attempting to find employment in an unstable economy. This book is especially designed for frustrated parents, anxious students, bewildered professors and educators, and those who deeply care for college graduates. Dr. Daryl Green and Mr. William Bailey offer an entertaining and delightful discussion to help your audience increase their chances for future employment.

(Paperback: 100 pages, ISBN: 978-1460925102, Kindle: 100 pages, ASIN: B005H41J7M, DVD: 26 minutes, ASIN: B001FB423G, Workbook Paperback: 42 pages, ISBN: 978-1490430072, Kindle Workbook: 41 pages, ASIN: B00DY8SG3I)

More Than a Conqueror: Achieving Personal Fulfillment in Government Service, co-authored with wife Estraletta, provides a message about how to take positive steps in achieving your goals while in government service. However, many individuals will be able to benefit from this book. In More than a Conqueror, you will (a) go beyond your self-imposed limitation by breaking the barrier of your self-doubt and (b) protect and cultivate your life in order to bring forth the best you can in your generation. (Paperback: 76 pages, ISBN: 978-0971400887)

My Cup Runneth Over: Setting Goals for Single Parents and Working Couples guides families in setting goals for themselves. Daryl and his wife have first-hand experience on this subject, both working full-time jobs and raising three active children. This book uses a new management process called Meshing™. The book is very different from most family books, focusing more on practical solutions. Daryl and his wife Estraletta have used their experience as managers in the government, nonprofit, and private business sectors to assist families in this country to do what they have done- take control of their families. Written in an informal, entertaining style, it provides information to families that give them HOPE. Creatively illustrated with graphics and charts, the book is also indexed for quick reference. It is essential reading for families in search of purpose.

Special Awards: January Book of the Month, The Larry Young Show 1998, Special Black History Award at Atkins Library, Featured on Heaven 600 (The Top Gospel Radio Station in the Country), (Paperback: 108 pages, ISBN: 978-1889745039, Audiobook: 978-1889745053, Audio CD: 30 minutes, ASIN: B001VH787E)

Selling by Objectives provides insight on how to create more sales during an economic crisis using seven key ingredients. The book provides practical solutions that today's organizations can easily digest and implement even in an unstable economy. This book is important not only for salespeople, but also for any professional involved in selling goods and services with a desire to be successful in the marketplace. Nonprofit organizations, business owners, college students, professors, entrepreneurs, and other sales organizations can benefit from this book.

(Paperback: 138 pages, ISBN: 978-1470054342)

DR. DARYL D. GREEN

Writing for Professionals provides individuals with authoritative writing tools. It offers strategies, practical guidelines, resources, and a host of suggestions to help with publishing goals. The advice in this book can be useful for a wide variety of professions, including business executives, teachers, scientists, engineers, attorneys, and many others.

(Paperback: 240 pages, ISBN: 978-1475152333)

Appendices

Additional Business Knowledge – Appendix A

Global Strategic Checklist – Appendix B

Green Top 50+ Promotional Strategies – Appendix C

Sample Marketing Strategy for Entrepreneurs – Appendix D

PEST and SWOT Analysis Checklist – Appendix E

Porter's Five Forces Template – Appendix E

APPENDIX

APPENDIX A

ADDITIONAL BUSINESS KNOWLEDGE

Learn about information designed to assist small businesses in competing on a global front. Contact the organizations for current information.

BOOKS/DOCUMENTS
Customer Relationship/Product Development
Consumer Behavior and the Practice of Marketing by Kenneth Runyon

Niche Marketing by Gordon Burgett

Positioning by Al Ries and Jack Trout

Publishing to Niche Markets by Gordon Burgett

Relationship Marketing by Regis McKenna

Entrepreneur/Small Business Enterprises
Entrepreneurship by Robert Hisrich, Michael Peters, and Dean Shepherd

Four Steps to Building a Profitable Business by Deborah Brown-Volkman

Going Part-time by Cindy Tolliver & Nancy Chambers

The Entrepreneur Guide by D. Brown

What is an Entrepreneurs by David Robinson

Global Market
Growing Your Business Globally by Robert Taft

Niche and Grow Rich by Jennifer and Peter Sander

Internet

101 Ways to Promote Your Web Site by Susan Sweeney

B2B by Michael J. Cunningham

Essential Business Tactics for the Net by Larry Chase & Eileen Shulock

Guerrilla Marketing Online Weapons by Jay Conrad Levinson and Charles Rubin

Internet World by Cliff Allen

Net Gain by John Hagell III

Net Worth by John Hagell III

The Complete Small Business Internet Guide by Tom & Lori Heatherington

Winning Results with Google Adwords by Andrew Goodman

Marketing Resources

Basic Marketing by William Perreault, Jr. and E. Jerome McCarthy

Guerrilla Marketing by Jay Conrad Levinson

Knock Your Socks Off by Jay Conrad Levinson

Marketing Management by John Mullins, Orville Walker, Jr., and Harper Boyd, Jr.

Streetfighter Marketing by Jeff Slutsky

Promotion

101 Ways to Promote Yourself by Raleigh Pinksey

1001 Ways to Make More Money as a Speaker, Consultant, or Trainer by Lilly Walters

Complete Publicity Plans by Sandra Beckwith

Guerrilla Marketing Online Weapons by Jay Conrad Levinson and Charles Rubin

You Can Hype Anything by Raleigh Pinksey

MARKETING FOR PROFESSIONALS

Selling

Advanced Selling Strategies by Brian Tracy

Speaking

1001 Ways to Make More Money as a Speaker, Consultant, or Trainer by Lilly Walters

How to Make a Fortune from Public Speaking by Dr. Robert Anthony

Speak and Grow Rich by Dottie Walters and Lilly Walters

Strategic Thinking

Positive Turbulence by Stanley Gryskiewicz

The Portable MBA in Entrepreneurship by William Bygrave and Andrew Zacharakis

Growing Your Business Globally by Robert Taft

"Strategic Thinking" by Rex C. Mitchell, Ph.D. (paper, 2005)

WEBSITES FOR ENTREPRENUERS

Business Assistance

Business Planning Resource www.bplans.com

Entrepreneur.com www.entrepreneur.com

Fortune Small Business www.fortunesb.com

Home Business Research www.homebusinessresearch.com

Internal Revenue Service www.irs.gov

SCORE www.score.org

Smart Business www.smartbiz.com

Small Business Administration www.sba.gov

Working Solo www.workingsolo.com

Marketing Research & Analysis Tools

Free SWOT or PEST Analysis Template http://www.businessballs.com/pestanalysisfreetemplate.htm

The Marketing Teacher www.marketingteacher.com/Lessons

The World Wide Internet Usage http://www.internetworldstats.com/stats.htm

APPENDIX B

STRATEGIC THINKING FOR GLOBAL MARKETS

GLOBAL MARKETS

1. Determine your objectives in the market.

2. Do initial market research.

3. Understand the target country culture and infrastructure.

4. Analyze current and future competitors in the target country.

5. Analyze the political, economic, social, and technological impacts of your market entrance (called PEST Analysis).

MARKETING

1. Determine your SWOT—strengths, weaknesses, opportunities, and threat—in entering this market.

2. Determine how you are currently positioned in this market.

3. Evaluate how you will gain credibility in this global market with promotions.

4. Determine your distribution channel—how you will get your product/service to your customers.

5. Determine the adequacy of your suppliers or your supply chain management system.

6. Determine a price strategy for your product/service in the global market.

ORGANIZATIONAL STRUCTURE

1. Determine if changes are needed in organizational structure.

2. Develop a business and market plan to incorporate this global market.

3. Identify local key partners or alliances needed.

4. Determine any additional training needed.

5. Evaluate resources needed including manpower and technology.

FINANCING

1. Determine your financial readiness for launching your business globally.

2. Determine any additional financing for business internationally.

3. Determine profit margin goals.

4. Secure a network of financial advisors.

APPENDIX C

GREEN TOP 50+ PROMOTIONAL IDEAS

The promotion strategy will pursue an aggressive guerrilla marketing approach to secure the entrepreneur's position in the market. The primary method will be the use of digital formats and a large grassroots network growing by "word of mouth." The following are my top 50 low-cost, effective tools and roles to employ in building relationships with your consumers and gaining an advantage over your competition:

1) Creative company name.

2) Word of mouth.

3) Writing sections of book for paid magazine articles.

4) Adjunct professor at a college or university.

5) Advice as an international and national expert.

6) Message board or discussion board moderator.

7) Keynote speaker.

8) Lecturer at non-credit course (local college).

9) Webinar trainer/presenter.

10) Attractive business website.

11) Search engine listings.

12) Effective analysis of competition.

13) Chatrooms.

14) Barter of services.

15) Social Media Platforms like Facebook and Pinterest.

16) Local columnist.

17) Flyers.

18) Business cards with personal photo.

19) Seminars & workshops.

20) Amazon.com placement.

21) Article directory membership.

22) Google advertising programs.

23) Freelance writing.

24) Testimonials/endorsements.

25) Feature on local company newsletters.

26) Good media relations.

27) Community sponsor.

28) Published author of book.

29) Community relationships (work, church, etc.).

30) Awareness campaign.

31) Local newsletters.

32) Ethnic communities .

33) Discussion groups.

34) Email campaign such as *Constant Contact.*

35) Sponsorship of e-newsletter.

36) Free advice.

37) Customer loyalty program.

38) Contests.

39) Media kits.

40) Online media kit.

41) Media release campaign on websites, such as Prweb.com.

42) Master of ceremony.

43) Executive or life coach.

44) Flyers.

45) Sponsor an award.

46) Create an event.

47) Sponsor a contest.

48) Tradeshows.

49) Expert directories.

50) Networking.

51) Endorsements.

52) Community involvement.

53) Op-ed pages and commentaries.

54) Calendar listing.

55) Unique selling position.

56) Good slogan.

APPENDIX D

SAMPLE PROMOTION STRATEGY WITH PERFORMANCE MEASURES

Entrepreneurial Goals
Online Press Release
Submit monthly, on newsworthy activities around holidays.
Send out tips or best books list.
Measures
Monthly increase of website links (see Google).
Increase in media interviews.

Business Website update
Make additions to keep website interesting.
Ask the Experts (email to afamilyvision@att.net).
List of Services.
Measures
Monthly increase in email traffic.
Monthly increase in services rendered.

Relevant Newsgroups
Conduct research and relationship as an online expert (business, leadership, working sites, etc.).
Maintain an ongoing relationship via email.

Measures
Monthly increase in email traffic on website.
Monthly increase of clients.

Digital Press Kit
Develop digital press kit for grassroots campaign.
Measures
Increase in book sales.
Increase in website traffic.
Increase in direct consulting services.

Appendix E

PEST Analysis

Purpose: A PEST Analysis allows a small business to analyze a market by reviewing the political, economical, socio-cultural, and technological factors of a given country. A PEST evaluation is similar to a STEEP (socio-cultural, technological, economical, environmental, and political) evaluation. This allows the entrepreneur to carefully evaluate a business opportunity while also reviewing his or her risks. Here are a few factors to analyze before entering a global market:

Political Factors

- What is the stability of the country's government?

- How will the government policies (regulations, taxes, etc.) impact your business?

- What is the government's position on ethical conduct in business transactions?

- What is the government's position on its economy?

- What is the government's trade relationship with the US or other Western countries?

Economic Factors

- What is the economic climate of the country?

- What is the level of inflation?

- What is the country's employment level per capita?

- What is the country's debt with other countries such as the US?

- What is the financial situation of the country's banking industry?

- What are the long-term prospects for the economy's Gross Domestic Product (GDP) per capita?

Socio-Cultural Factors

- What is the people's attitude toward foreign products and services, especially from the US?

- What is the dominant religion?

- How does language impact the delivery of goods and services to the market?

- What is the dominant language?

- Are people exposed to Western culture or isolated from it?

- How much leisure time do consumers have?

- What roles do men and women have in this society?

- What is the age of the population?
- How do children impact the purchasing habits of parents?
- How is wealth distributed among the people?

Technological Factors

- How is technology accepted in this society?
- Does technology allow for goods and services to be made more cheaply and to better quality standards?
- Does technology offer customers and businesses more innovative goods and services, such as cell phones or Internet?
- Does technology offer businesses new ways to communicate with each other?
- Does technology improve the quality of life for the citizens of this country?

PEST Analysis

Political Factors	Economic Factors
Socio-cultural Factors	Technological Factors

Source: www.marketingteacher.com

SWOT Analysis

Purpose: A SWOT Analysis allows a small business to evaluate itself while also analyzing the external environment as it relates to opportunities and threats. Businesses should be careful to distinguish their business strengths and weaknesses differently in a global market than in a domestic one.

Environment	Positive	Negative
Internal	Strengths	Weaknesses
External	Opportunities	Threats

SWOT Analysis Example

HELPFUL	HARMFUL
Strengths	**Weaknesses**
Availability of more faculty in the immediate geographic area Availability of more students in immediate area Brand name (recognized across the country) Credentials and experience of faculty Dedicated faculty/staff DOE national lab and state university nearby Multi-cultural student body	Customer image Deteriorating facilities and infrastructure Formality of operations Financial debt Lack of a competitive curriculum Lack of accreditation Lack of accountability Lack of physical security Low involvement of faculty in organization Low morale amidst stakeholders
Opportunities	**Threats**
Alliance with state and private institutions Acquiring bright new faculty (use of perks, titles, etc.) Alliance with state and private institutions Community outreach Developmental center for emerging leadership Distance learning application Entrepreneurial partnerships and spin-offs	Breach of security with severe consequences Cash flow issues (payroll, debt payments, etc.) Deteriorating facilities and infrastructure Decreased revenue streams Faculty and staff departure Financial debt Liabilities with no insurance Major lawsuits Market changes More intense competition

APPENDIX F

Porter's Five Forces Analysis

Purpose: Porter's Five Forces Analysis allows entrepreneurs or small businesses to determine if a market is favorable or attractive (See Figure 1). Entrepreneurs should complete the template by putting 2-3 key descriptions of the five forces (i.e. substitution, buyer power, supplier power, new entrants, and competitive rivalry). Rank each element as High – H, Medium, or Low –L.

PORTER'S FIVE FORCES MODEL

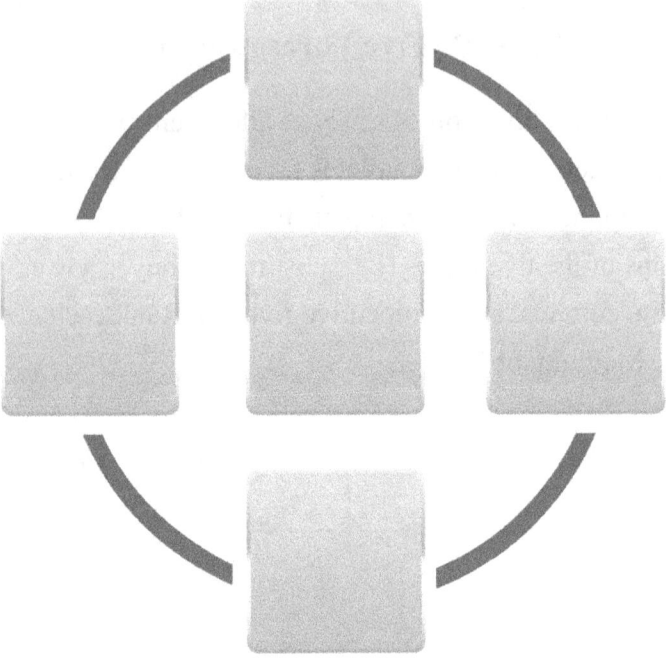

This figure is based on Dr. Michael Porter's Five Forces of Competitive Position Model

INDEX

Brand 39,70,

Business xi, 2, 3, 6, 42, 43, 46, 47, 48, 51,52, 55, 60, 63,65, 67, 69,71

Burgett 8,37,51

Gordon 8,37,51,

Buyers 6,7,8,11,12,19,20,26,39,40,

Competition v, xii, 2, 8, 13, 14, 15, 16, 17, 18, 20, 21, 26, 27, 28, 29, 31, 39, 40, 59, 60, 70

Competitors, 13, 26, 39

Customers, 6, 40

Customizing, 8, 40

Daft, Richard, 15

Entrepreneurship, 11, 37, 51

Entrepreneur, 37, 51

Expanding, 8

Globalization, 51

Green, Daryl, iii, 35

Gryskiewicz, Stanley, 23, 37, 53

Guerrilla marketing, 24, 37

Hisrich, Robert, 37, 51

Keller, Kevin, 18, 19, 20, 37

Kotler, Phillip, 18, 19, 20, 37

Levinson, Jay Conrad, 37, 39, 52

Market, 5, 23

Marketing, 23, 40, 53

Marketing environment, 32

Millennials, 13, 15

PEST analysis, 55, 57, 65

Place, 16, 24, 33

Positioning, 27, 51

Porter, Michael, 17, 18, 71

Porter's Five Forces, 49, 71

Price, 7, 16, 20, 58

Product, 1, 2, 8, 31

Product development, 5, 51

Promotion, 28, 49

Ries, Al, 27, 51

SWOT analysis, 49, 69, 70

Target market, 7, 8, 10, 12, 26, 29, 40

Trout, Jack, 27, 51

Unique selling proposition, 7

Value, 6, 40

www.ingramcontent.com/pod-product-compliance
Lightning Source LLC
Chambersburg PA
CBHW060407190526
45169CB00002B/794